OUTSIDE THE
BOX,
WITHIN THE
CUBE

1001 Quotes About the Art of Being a Good Teammate

LANCE LOYA

CAGER HAUS
PUBLISHING

ISBN-13: 978-1-7325505-9-9

www.coachloya.com

Design and publishing by Cager Haus.

For Laken and Lakota…may you always be good teammates.

Introduction

Who doesn't enjoy a good quote? Quotes inspire us to become better versions of ourselves. They lift us up when we feel down, guide us when we feel lost, and empower us when we feel constrained.

I grew up around sports, where quotes are ubiquitous. The locker room walls of my youth were adorned with motivational quotes. I loved it when my coaches worked famous quotes into their pre-game speeches.

Failure to prepare is preparing to fail. You miss 100 percent of the shots you don't take. It's not the size of the dog in the fight, it's the size of the fight in the dog.

This book is a collection of quotes about the art of being a good teammate. My world revolves around this subject. I am completely consumed with it. Every waking hour of my day is devoted to learning more about what makes these special team members tick.

A few years ago, I started sharing what I learned about good teammates on my social media pages—140 characters at a time. As it turned out, the limitation proved to be the perfect length to dispense my discoveries. While I occasionally shared a quote from Wooden, Gandhi, or Churchill, my good teammate insights always seemed to get the bigger response. The good teammate insights I shared make up the 1,001 quotes that follow.

I realized early in my journey of discovery that good teammates think differently. They think *outside the box*. Most people are instinctively selfish. Most people think *What's best for me?* That way of thinking creates team problems. Good teammates are selfless. They think *What's best for my team?* Their way of thinking solves team problems. However, their approach is confined by a strict adherence to a rigid set of guiding principles—their team's core values.

The phrase *outside the box* is a cliché, originating from a human resource exercise designed to gauge creative thinking. Potential hires were asked to connect nine dots by drawing four straight lines, without ever lifting their pencil from the paper. The only way to solve the puzzle was to extend the lines outside the nine-dot square/box. Hence, the phrase *thinking outside the box.*

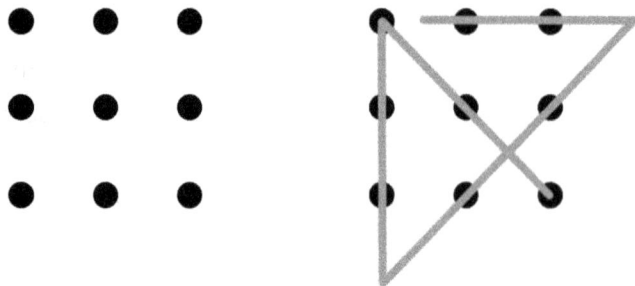

To understand the mindset of good teammates, consider their creative approach to solving problems as being represented by a two-dimensional shape—a square/box. Encompassing this shape is a three-dimensional cube. The cube is defined by the team's core values (i.e., loyalty, commitment, honesty, etc.). In other words, good teammates may think differently, but their actions never stray from their team's core values. Or, as the title of this book suggests, *good teammates think outside the box but act within the cube.*

Does that thought resonate with you? If so, then you have picked up the right book. My hope is that these quotes inspire you to become a better teammate or help you inspire someone you know to become a better teammate. Why? Because the world cannot have too many good teammates.

-1-

Good teammates think outside the box but act within the cube.

-2-

Selfishness sinks ships: championships, friendships, partnerships, relationships, even leaderships.

-3-

Good teammates are not immobilized by fear.

-4-

Teamwork might make the dream work, but teammates make the team work.

-5-

Kindness leads to kinship.

-6-

Teams are never handicapped by unselfishness.

-7-

You learn from everyone you meet. Sometimes it's what to do. Sometimes it's what *not* to do.

-8-

Good teammates understand the only real limits are the ones they set for themselves.

-9-

You don't have to move mountains to be a good teammate, but your actions may inspire others to.

-10-

Energy and vitality are essential to being a good teammate.

-11-

Good teammates determine the team's ultimate success.

-12-

Good teammates despise whining.

-13-

Whoever said nice guys finish last was too impatient. In the end, nice guys are the only ones who finish.

-14-

Organize your life around the idea of being a good teammate.

-15-

Good teammates refuse to compromise what they know to be right for anyone.

-16-

Be a good teammate…because it's the right thing to do.

-17-

Good teammates are flexible on many things, but ethics and truth are not among them.

-18-

Good teammates turn losses into learning experiences.

-19-

The kindness you extend to your teammates is directly proportional to the respect you have for your team.

-20-

Good teammates are the glue that holds the team together.

-21-

The solution to getting better involves a simple equation: BUY IN + EFFORT = IMPROVEMENT.

-22-

Good teammates always take the high road, even if it's the road less traveled.

-23-

Manners still matter to good teammates.

-24-

Good teammates make others feel appreciated.

-25-

Teamwork doesn't happen without good teammates.

-26-

Good teammates don't confuse compliance for commitment.

-27-

Three Things a Player Needs from a Coach: 1.) Someone to encourage me, 2.) Someone to hold me accountable, and 3.) Someone to model good behavior.

-28-

Good teammates always find a way.

-29-

The sacrifice you make today may become the difference you make tomorrow.

-30-

Good teammates know extra effort is always worth it.

-31-

Sometimes small contributions have huge impacts.

-32-

When you love, you care. When you care, you love.

-33-

Admitting your mistakes is not a sign of weakness.

-34-

Bad leaders turn loyalty into resentment because they don't recognize the commitment.

-35-

Good teammates strive to improve a little every day.

-36-

Prioritize your teams. Not every team you belong to (*sports, work, family, friends, clubs, etc.*) is deserving of the same amount of time.

-37-

Good teammates gauge their value by the impact they have on others.

-38-

Seek what is best for your team, not what's best for you.

-39-

Inner peace comes from doing the right things.

-40-

Good teammates put the needs of the team ahead of their individual agendas.

-41-

If life gives you a spoon and your competition a shovel, don't waste time complaining. Dig faster.

-42-

Good teammates discipline themselves.

-43-

Real winners find joy in being good teammates.

-44-

Good teammates must be initiators of change yet upholders of culture.

-45-

Want to improve your team? ELIMINATE DRAMA.

-46-

Good teammates don't allow others to make them feel inferior.

-47-

Attitude is everything to a good teammate.

-48-

Good teammates know it's better to see your game than hear your game. Talk less. Act more.

-49-

Relationships always matter to good teammates.

-50-

Good teammates bounce back after a defeat. They don't stay knocked down.

-51-

If you have to cheat to get ahead, you're not getting ahead.

-52-

Your commitment to your role may define you, but it doesn't have to confine you.

-53-

Good teammates strive to improve a little every day.

-54-

Never let your fears dictate your options.

-55-

Good teammates despise laziness.

-56-

When you're part of a team, your choices impact everyone else on that team.

-57-

Set your goals. Set your mind. Erase your limits.

-58-

The secret to happiness is finding purpose. The secret to finding purpose is finding something to serve.

-59-

Good teammates are prepared for when their chance comes.

-60-

To experience the treasure of the WE gear, you must be willing to abandon the allure of the ME gear.

-61-

Good teammates radiate positivity.

-62-

The extent of a good teammate's loyalty is limited by one guiding principle: Loyalty above all…except honor.

-63-

Good teammates are the key to progress.

-64-

What is good for the team is good for you.

-65-

Good teammates don't hide in the shadows. They have the courage to step into the light.

-66-

Three ways to avoid criticism: 1.) Do nothing, 2.) Say nothing, and 3.) Be nothing.

-67-

Good teammates don't trade long-term goals for short-term gratification.

-68-

Work hard. Play hard. But don't ever be hard.

-69-

Good teammates are committed to functioning as one single unit.

-70-

Good teammates let it go. They don't dwell on their failures; they learn from them and move on.

-71-

Sore losers miss out on the opportunity to learn from a loss.

-72-

Good teammates turn doubt into motivation.

-73-

If you want your teammates to respect you, you must first respect the team.

-74-

Good teammates know how to empower others.

-75-

You don't have to win to be a good teammate, but being a good teammate gives you the best chance to win.

-76-

Good teammates always rise to the occasion.

-77-

Leaders are teammates too.

-78-

Good teammates are the common denominator of every successful group.

-79-

The best motivational act you can do for a teammate is to listen with sincerity.

-80-

Good teammates are more powerful than they realize.

-81-

You can't have an inconsistent attitude and expect to be a consistent player.

-82-

Nothing prevents the teams most talented players from also being the team's most talented teammates.

-83-

Good teammates give more than what is expected.

-84-

Being a good teammate is a talent that doesn't require talent.

-85-

Good teammates are committed to becoming masters of their roles.

-86-

Authenticity leads to trust.

-87-

Good players are a dime a dozen. Good teammates are priceless.

-88-

Good teammates laugh with you, not at you.

-89-

Build up your teammates, tear down your competition.

-90-

A leader doesn't have to convince a good teammate to get on board.

-91-

Good teammates make an effort to try to see the good in people when they feel blinded by the bad.

-92-

You don't have to change everything to be a better teammate, but being a better teammate could change everything.

-93-

A good teammate is neither arrogant nor ignorant.

-94-

Good teammates must be willing to let go of the things that stunt their growth.

-95-

Good teammates don't get distracted by pettiness.

-96-

Be a good teammate today…your future self will thank you.

-97-

Selfishness will destroy a team quicker than any opponent.

-98-

Three ways to be a better teammate: 1.) Care more, 2.) Share more, and 3.) Listen more.

-99-

Good teammates abandon habits that hinder.

-100-

Above and beyond...Two words that are synonymous with being a good teammate.

-101-

Good teammates share the accolades.

-102-

Four steps to building a winning team: 1.) Establish leadership, 2.) Set goals, 3.) Inject the good teammate mindset, and 4.) Achieve success.

-103-

Good teammates act now. They don't wait for problems to become emergencies.

-104-

Teams succeed when they are comprised of good teammates.

-105-

Good teammates are people of action.

-106-

Never be too proud to laugh at yourself.

-107-

Good teammates make their decisions based on what is best for their team.

-108-

Win, lose, or draw…always support your teammates.

-109-

Good teammates understand their choices affect everyone on their team.

-110-

If you really want to find meaning in your life, start helping others find meaning in theirs.

-111-

Good teammates aren't afraid to go against the grain.

-112-

It's not what you do *with* your teammates, it's what you do *for* your teammates.

-113-

Good teammates bring their "A-game"...*every* game.

-114-

Small victories lead to big rewards.

-115-

Good teammates aspire to inspire.

-116-

Good teammates don't focus on *me*. They focus on *we*.

-117-

On the best teams, the gap between rookies and veterans is filled with sharing.

-118-

Good teammates must be gardeners and routinely rip out the weeds in their team garden.

-119-

Don't get bogged down trying to figure out who's right, focus on what's right.

-120-

Good teammates hear and adhere to the team's rules.

-121-

Good teammates are what allow the team to defeat its competition, not itself.

-122-

When you can't control the situation, control your attitude.

-123-

Good teammates do not defend their mistakes. They learn from them.

-124-

Good teammates are always emotionally attached.

-125-

Courage is contagious.

-126-

Good teammates don't allow their woes to contaminate their team's flow.

-127-

Put your effort into building the teammate and the teamwork will take care of itself.

-128-

Good teammates focus on what they *can* control.

-129-

Your leader is responsible for strategy. You're responsible for your execution.

-130-

Good teammates don't ask "What's in it for me?"

-131-

Good teammates inspire through their actions, not their intentions.

-132-

Be the guardian of your team's standards.

-133-

Team leaders experience their biggest failures when their teams' biggest personality isn't a good teammate.

-134-

It often takes as much effort to complain about a problem as it does to fix it.

-135-

Good teammates dream big and work hard to make that dream a reality.

-136-

Caring leads to passion. Passion leads to solutions.

-137-

Good teammates bring out the good in others.

-138-

Good teammates are what bring serenity to a turbulent team.

-139-

Empower your teammates by believing in them.

-140-

Good teammates are more concerned with getting it right than who is to blame.

-141-

Good teammates are laborers. They build bridges and break down barriers.

-142-

A friendly ear can turn you into a good teammate.

-143-

Good teammates don't blame, shame, or complain.

-144-

Good teammates must have the courage to speak up, but the discipline to listen.

-145-

Sometimes being a good teammate means laying it all on the line.

-146-

Good teammates never lose sight of the big picture.

-147-

Be more concerned with earning respect than being annoyed with perceived disrespect.

-148-

Good teammates are not deterred by disasters. They are willing to pick up the pieces and start over.

-149-

When you raise your energy level, you lift your team.

-150-

Good teammates are never stingy with compliments.

-151-

Aspire higher...it will help your team grow.

-152-

Good teammates know what they stand for, and what they won't stand for.

-153-

Choose your battles wisely.

-154-

Good teammates stand up for those who cannot stand up for themselves.

-155-

When the conversation takes a negative tone, good teammates become tone deaf.

-156-

Good teammates are filled with grit...Don't give in!

-157-

Self-control is the foundation of a good teammate.

-158-

If you are going to be a good teammate, you have got to be ALL IN.

-159-

Good teammates doing good things is what bonds a team.

-160-

Always remember: The gold lies in the grind. Persistence pays.

-161-

Good teammates are able to turn a setback into a comeback.

-162-

The willingness to confront is what differentiates a good guy from a good teammate.

-163-

Good teammates may not know the way, but they always know where they're going.

-164-

On the best teams, everyone leads. Everyone is a good teammate.

-165-

Good teammates look for reasons, not excuses.

-166-

Sometimes being a good teammate means being a good example.

-167-

Be the kind of teammate you wish you had.

-168-

Good teammates must be masters of their attitude.

-169-

Win/win situations have a way of producing good teammates.

-170-

The ability to keep calm during intense encounters is a trademark of a good teammate. Their calmness puts others at ease.

-171-

Good teammates are winners, not whiners.

-172-

Courage is the mark of being a good teammate.

-173-

"Just be yourself" is bad advice if you are not instinctively a good teammate.

-174-

Good teammates value the journey, not just the destination.

-175-

Never criticize before you empathize.

-176-

Good teammates invest time into building relationships.

-177-

Grit allows good teammates to survive the grind.

-178-

Good teammates must have an intolerance for selfishness.

-179-

Three reasons good teammates communicate: 1.) To congratulate, 2.) To console, and 3.) To confront. If what you have to say doesn't fit into one of those three categories, you shouldn't say it.

-180-

Good teammates are fully committed…to all they do.

-181-

A kind heart opens doors and breaks down barriers.

-182-

Good teammates inspire you to keep going when you are tempted to give up.

-183-

Good teammates must be masters of their emotions.

-184-

Be committed. Don't abandon ship just because the sea gets a little rough.

-185-

Good teammates radiate enthusiasm, even when they don't feel enthusiastic.

-186-

Jealousy erodes the team.

-187-

Good teammates possess the unique ability to simply enjoy without complaint.

-188-

Good teammates must be self-starters.

-189-

The best teammates live by a six-word philosophy: serve the needs of the team.

-190-

Good teammates help us go where we cannot take ourselves.

-191-

There's nothing quite like the healing power of a good teammate's approval.

-192-

Good teammates hang on when others let go.

-193-

The willingness to be happy for someone else's accomplishment is the mark of a good teammate.

-194-

Shallow teammates lead to deep problems.

-195-

When it comes to gossip, good teammates must have selective hearing and not engage.

-196-

Good teammates believe.

-197-

Do you make your teammates better? Good teammates do.

-198-

Good teammates handle adversity. They don't let it handle them.

-199-

A good teammate's strongest muscle is his heart.

-200-

Good teammates can be skeptical, but not cynical.

-201-

Good teammates take action. They don't wait for problems to solve themselves.

-202-

When your team's best player is also your team's best teammate, amazing things happens.

-203-

Good teammates lead by example.

-204-

If your objective is to find success, then your strategy should be to serve.

-205-

Good teammates never hesitate to confront a team problem.

-206-

The Golden Rule for being a good teammate: Put the team ahead of yourself.

-207-

Good teammates do not allow adversity to alter their attitude.

-208-

It's easier to be selfish than to sacrifice. Good teammates sacrifice—for the good of their team.

-209-

Good teammates have ambition. They're obsessed with finding a better way of doing things.

-210-

Knowledge was meant to be shared, not stored.

-211-

If being a good teammate was easy, everybody would already be one.

-212-

Leave a legacy by being a good teammate.

-213-

Good teammates are committed to the process.

-214-

Be willing to reset your weaknesses with your week. Monday's are perfect for fresh starts.

-215-

Good teammates are the foundation of a house built for success.

-216-

Good teammates must be proactive.

-217-

Sometimes the kindest thing you can do for your teammates is to teach them how to do it for themselves.

-218-

Good teammates don't stay knocked down. They always bounce back.

-219-

Jealousy is a foreign word to a good teammate.

-220-

Good teammates have a way of enjoying the moment.

-221-

When you love your teammates, the team loves you.

-222-

Good teammates want to enrich, not be rich. They're motivated by the accumulation of internal wealth.

-223-

Doesn't matter if you see yourself as a leader or a follower, you still need to be a good teammate.

-224-

Good teammates forge ahead when others fall behind.

-225-

It often takes as much effort to complain about an issue, as it does to fix it.

-226-

Good teammates electrify the room with their energy.

-227-

Sometimes being a good teammate means nothing more than being a good listener.

-228-

Do big things by caring about the little things.

-229-

Nothing about bullying is acceptable to a good teammate.

-230-

Good teammates must have patience with the process.

-231-

If you face one fear today, you become stronger. And so does your team.

-232-

Good teammates never quit on their team.

-233-

Good teammates raise their stock by lifting others, not by putting others down.

-234-

Wisdom evolves through a combination of experience and a commitment to not make the same mistake twice.

-235-

Good teammates realize that failure is never final.

-236-

Good teammates grow up to be good fathers and mothers.

-237-

High fives are the currency of a good teammate.

-238-

Good teammates crave feedback because they want to get better.

-239-

That which is not confronted festers until it fails. Deal with little problems before they become big problems.

-240-

Good teammates must have faith in the mission and faith though the journey.

-241-

Pursuing your purpose leads to enlightenment.

-242-

Good teammates are as ethically fit as they are physically fit.

-243-

Good teammates fight until the end. They don't give up and they don't give in.

-244-

Love your teammates as you love yourself.

-245-

The root of a splintered team always lies in the formation of a clique.

-246-

Being on a team, void of any good teammates, is like digging a ditch with a spoon, while the competition has a shovel.

-247-

Good teammates promise without forgetting.

-248-

Individual goals should take a backseat to team goals.

-249-

One person deciding to be a good teammate can change the team's entire culture.

-250-

Good teammates precede good teamwork.

-251-

You must know when to give a teammate a pat on the backside, and when to give 'em a kick.

-252-

Good teammates must be honest with others, as well as honest with themselves.

-253-

You either help your team's culture or you hurt it. There is no in between.

-254-

Good teammates must be beacons of hope.

-255-

Become independent of the things that are holding you back from being a better teammate.

-256-

Good teammates approach the future with a plan.

-257-

Even when their energy tank appears empty, good teammates somehow manage to find more.

-258-

Good teammates cannot be pretentious.

-259-

When you invest in personal development, you make your team better.

-260-

Good teammates respond when others repulse.

-261-

Effort shouldn't be attached to your opponent. Good teammates give a consistent effort, regardless of who they face.

-262-

Good teammates put others at ease with their presence.

-263-

An investment in a teammate is an investment in the team.

-264-

Good teammates choose their battles wisely.

-265-

The talent of being a good teammate is the most valued talent on the team.

-266-

Good teammates know that speaking up may have consequences, but so might remaining silent.

-267-

Bad teammates hoard. Good teammates share.

-268-

Good teammates listen without interrupting and speak without accusing.

-269-

Dream big. Act bigger.

-270-

Good teammates know how to roll up their sleeves and go to work.

-271-

Gratitude opens doors that scorn cannot.

-272-

Good teammates have a positive mindset.

-273-

Good teammates are predictable. Their consistency puts people at ease.

-274-

You must prune the toxic branches of your tree before they cause irreversible damage.

-275-

Good teammates appreciate what others are good at.

-276-

The quality of a teammate is seen in the standards they set for themself.

-277-

Good teammates learn from the past, live in the present, and are excited about the future.

-278-

Reach for new heights...then reach down and lift someone else up with you.

-279-

Good teammates look to grow opportunities.

-280-

Care about your teammates so much that their pain becomes your pain.

-281-

Good teammates don't let their mistakes define them.

-282-

Have you asked a teammate today: "How can I help you?"

-283-

Good teammates keep the team grounded during good times and stable during bad times.

-284-

Find your life's purpose and then pursue it with passion.

-285-

Good teammates are always ready.

-286-

Good teammates know how to turn negatives into positives.

-287-

Asking *why?* is important, because it is what helps you understand intent and facilitates your ability to solve the problem.

-288-

Sometimes a smile is a good teammate's most influential tool.

-289-

Good teammates share.

-290-

Good teammates are not afraid to speak up.

-291-

Be optimistic. It will inspire your teammates.

-292-

Good teammates stand up for what is right, not what is popular.

-293-

The best coaches teach to the heart with the heart. The best teammates serve to the heart with the heart.

-294-

Good teammates understand that good communication is a two-way street. Listening is as important as speaking.

-295-

Good teammates put others before themselves.

-296-

In a world where you can be anything, be a good teammate.

-297-

Good teammates change the team through their actions, not their opinions.

-298-

Do not let your ego get in the way of you being a good teammate.

-299-

Good teammates do not operate on assumptions.

-300-

Good teammates control their emotions. They don't let their emotions control them.

-301-

If you can't get their attention, you won't get their connection.

-302-

Good teammates despise gossip.

--303-

GIVE UP and GIVE IN are never options for a good teammate.

-304-

Good teammates must have the ability to be happy for another teammate's success.

-305-

Good teammates understand that mediocre efforts lead to mediocre results.

-306-

You must have a passion for your purpose.

-307-

Good teammates walk the walk before they talk the talk.

-308-

If teamwork is your destination, then trust must be your vehicle.

-309-

A coach's words are like tattoos on a player's soul. Be mindful with what you say because even removed tattoos leave scars.

-310-

Good teammates have a *team-first* mentality.

-311-

Act now. *Someday* may be too late..

-312-

When it comes to effort, your attitude should be: *Whatever it takes.*

-313-

Good teammates hustle.

-314-

Be a uniter, not a divider.

-315-

Don't allow your woes to hinder your team's flow.

-316-

Good teammates may not always know the way...but they always know the *why*.

-317-

It doesn't take talent to be a good teammate, but being a good teammate is a talent.

-318-

Be inspired by the success of your teammates. It's the path to finding your own success.

-319-

Good teammates are able to look each other in the eye and speak the truth.

-320-

Never underestimate how influential a good teammate can be on a team's culture.

-321-

Teamwork doesn't happen without the infusion of good teammates.

-322-

WE > ME

-323-

Good teammates are always the last to surrender.

-324-

Good teammates work to get everyone on the same page.

-325-

You don't have to play sports to be a good teammate.

-326-

Good teammates concentrate on their execution and their effort. Not their outcome.

-327-

A bad teammate does what he wants to do. A good teammate does what he has to do.

-328-

Good teammates freely give praise and credit.

-329-

Your culture: Create it. Nurture it. And most importantly, fight for it.

-330-

Good teammates are what hold a team together during tough times.

-331-

A teambuster's first question is always "What's in it for me?"

-332-

To avoid the pitfalls of self-pity, good teammates must view challenges as temporary inconveniences.

-333-

We need to have a thirst for knowledge, but a willingness to share what we learn.

-334-

Good teammates take initiative.

-335-

Continuous learning is part of being a good teammate.

-336-

Good teammates do the right thing even when no one is watching.

-337-

Teammates who embrace their role are what make the difference between good and great teams.

-338-

Good teammates expect the unexpected.

-339-

Looking for motivation? Do it for your team. No purer form of motivation exists.

-340-

Good teammates seek the good in others.

-341-

Teamwork doesn't happen without having the mindset of a good teammate.

-342-

A toxic teammate leads to a toxic team.

-343-

Good teammates are hidden treasures, seek them out and enjoy their riches.

-344-

Don't let your ego get in the way of your ambition.

-345-

Good teammates know the storm will eventually pass and that's why they ride it out.

-346-

When it comes to enthusiasm, good teammates are fountains, not drains.

-347-

Sometimes small acts of kindness produce the biggest results.

-348-

Good teammates work with a sense of urgency.

-349-

A good teammate's daily objective: Be awesome today.

-350-

Serving leads to purpose. Purpose leads to happiness. Happiness leads to wholeness.

-351-

Good teammates have an intolerance for selfishness.

-352-

Good teammates are willing to sacrifice for the sanctity of their team.

-353-

Do something kind for someone who can never repay you. It will build your heart's resume.

-354-

Good teammates embrace the habit of always wanting to get better.

-355-

A good teammate is someone who knows all about you and still likes you.

-356-

If you lose a teammate due to your integrity, you made your team stronger.

-357-

Good teammates respect the team's time.

-358-

Good teammates check their ego at the door.

-359-

Sometimes being strong means being a good listener.

-360-

Three effective good teammate strategies: 1.) Arrive earlier, 2.) Work harder, and 3.) Stay longer.

-361-

Cruel words will stain a relationship.

-362-

Good teammates do not hesitate to speak up when others remain silent.

-363-

Too many fixate on what, when, where, and how. Good teammates focus on why.

-364-

Good teammates don't need alibis.

-365-

Giving a person responsibility without authority is setting that person up for failure. If you can't trust them, don't entrust them.

-366-

Good teammates cannot be deterred by failure.

-367-

Know your teammates. And let your teammates know you.

-368-

There's no better reward than being known as your team's best teammate.

-369-

Good teammates must hold themselves to the highest standards.

-370-

Drama erodes the team's culture.

-371-

When the driver of your team is a toxic teammate, a crash is inevitable.

-372-

Good teammates have infectious qualities.

-373-

Good teammates contribute when others deplete.

-374-

Good teammates die empty. They exhaust their energy, enthusiasm, love, care, passion, etc.

-375-

Loyalty is something you give regardless of what you get back.

-376-

The most important ingredient in teamwork is the teammate.

-377-

Good teammates don't get people to be on board by tearing them down.

-378-

Go out of your way to help a teammate in need. It will be worth it.

-379-

Good teammates try to do it right the first time, because they know they may not have time to do it over.

-380-

Toxicity tanks teams.

-381-

Good teammates may bend, but they never break.

-382-

The problem with participation trophies is they put a premium on awards and not the process. Good teammates cherish the process.

-383-

Have trust. Build trust. Earn trust. But don't ever lose trust.

-384-

Good teammates maintain balance in their life.

-385-

Good teammates bring value to the team through their values.

-386-

Good teammates believe when others doubt.

-387-

Teamwork may break down, but a good teammate never does.

-388-

Good teammates are the bridge between where the team used to be and where it wants to be.

-389-

Here's the magic formula for being a good teammate: Team first, self second.

-390-

Good teammates are what mend a fractured team.

-391-

Don't be discouraged by doubters.

-392-

Good teammates are willing to listen to others.

-393-

Sometimes the kindest thing you can do for a teammate is to confront the waywardness.

-394-

Good teammates understand their attitude is contagious.

-395-

It's amazing what you can endure when you have the support of your teammates.

-396-

When you're part of a team, it doesn't matter how badly you want it. You've got to get others to want it too.

-397-

Be above your team's pettiness.

-398-

Having BUY IN is good, but convincing others to BUY IN is even better.

-399-

Good teammates are the magical ingredient in every successful team.

-400-

Your ability to be a good teammate influences your team's capacity to have teamwork.

-401-

Good teammates know how to communicate with their words and their body language.

-402-

Your loyalty comes from your values.

-403-

Good teammates are always thankful for their blessings.

-404-

Sometimes it is better to lose an argument than to destroy the relationship.

-405-

Good teammates always consider the repercussions before they act.

-406-

Good teammates know life is not a popularity contest.

-407-

Doing something kind for someone who can never repay you is like making a deposit in your soul's bank.

-408-

When teammates perspire, they inevitably inspire.

-409-

Good teammates pay it forward.

-410-

When you fall down in life, be loyal to the person who helps you up.

-411-

Good teammates plan thoroughly, but remain flexible.

-412-

One person deciding to be a better teammate can change a team's entire culture.

-413-

Good teammates reinforce the team's culture.

-414-

Good teammates understand they represent more than just themselves.

-415-

The enthusiasm level of good teammates can illuminate the darkest of rooms.

-416-

Good teammates are humble.

-417-

Good teammates cannot allow their vices to alter their values.

-418-

When the team wins, you win. When you win, the team wins.

-419-

Good teammates always tell the truth…even when it's hard.

-420-

When you are surrounded by good teammates, you always have a chance.

-421-

Good teammates must have the courage to speak the truth when others won't.

-422-

When you share, you show you care. Good teammates share.

-423-

Good teammates take pride in filling the role their team needs from them.

-424-

Good teammates have the ability to make you smile even when you have tears in your eyes.

-425-

Good teammates steady the ground on which the team walks.

-426-

Good teammates ask themselves "What's best for the team?" when weighing their options.

-427-

Make an effort to understand the intent of the action before chastising the offender.

-428-

Teammates are like links in a chain. Don't be the weak link that allows the chain to break.

-429-

Unselfish teammates lead to unexpected victories.

-430-

Be a *teambuilder*, not a *teambuster*.

-431-

Being trustworthy comes from being consistent.

-432-

Awareness of team morale is critical. Good teammates are always aware of how their team is doing.

-433-

Good teammates find a way to make those around them better.

-434-

No role is insignificant to someone who cares about the team.

-435-

Good teammates must forego self-centeredness.

-436-

Don't waste your time complaining about your role. Spend your time becoming a master of it.

-437-

Good teammates think ahead.

-438-

Good teammates are always the hardest working people on the team.

-439-

Make being a good teammate your life's theme.

-440-

Good teammates are always cognizant of the ripple effect of their decisions.

-441-

Good teammates make every minute count. They deplore wasted time.

-442-

Being empathetic is a way of listening without the need for words.

-443-

Good teammates expect the unexpected.

-444-

Just because you call a group a team doesn't make it a team.

-445-

Good teammates respect time.

-446-

Confidence you tell yourself. Arrogance you try to tell everybody else. Choose confidence, avoid arrogance.

-447-

Good teammates embody the Christmas spirit *every* day.

-448-

Sometimes being a good teammate means being the bigger person.

-449-

Be kind to your teammates. Kindness leads to connected. Connected teams have the greatest chance of experiencing success.

-450-

Good teammates want to impact, not impress.

-451-

Good teammates know *good enough* seldom is.

-452-

Want to be a hero? Be somebody's good teammate.

-453-

Good teammates must look for opportunities to make others feel involved.

-454-

Selfishness never leads to team success. Selflessness never leads to team failure.

-455-

Being a good teammate will be the skill that has the greatest impact on your life, career, and family.

-456-

Good teammates believe their word is their bond.

-457-

Sometimes, *what* is being said is secondary to *how* it is being said.

-458-

Cliques are mini-teams formed within the main team. Cliques destroy teams. Good teammates don't form teams of their own.

-459-

Good teammates elevate their status by caring.

-460-

Integrity is of paramount importance to a good teammate.

-461-

Good teammates consider things from every angle.

-462-

When it matters, you care. When you care, it matters.

-463-

Good teammates share. They give without remembering and receive without forgetting.

-464-

What challenges the team bonds the team.

-465-

Good teammates measure their success by what their team accomplished, not in how they looked.

-466-

Being a good teammate brings clarity to your choices.

-467-

Good teammates must know when to comfort and when to confront.

-468-

Loyalty is substantiated through words and actions.

-469-

Good teammates stand up for what's right, not what's popular.

-470-

An upbeat teammate lifts the team.

-471-

You have to check your pride at the door and concede to the role your team needs you to assume.

-472-

Good teammates share openly and willingly.

-473-

The ability to get along is an invaluable, yet too often underrated skill.

-474-

Forget about the doubters. Forge ahead anyway!

-475-

Good teammates are able to stay focused on the ultimate goal.

-476-

You build loyalty by telling the truth.

-477-

Good teammates must be able to foresee problems before they become tragedies.

-478-

A team is not a family until everybody is on board.

-479-

Good teammates must strive to be consistent without being rigid. When people aren't listening, good teammates adjust the way the message is delivered.

-480-

Good teammates use their ME to elevate their WE.

-481-

Everything matters. Pay attention to the details.

-482-

Good teammates are humble, kind, and generous...and also fiercely competitive.

-483-

When good teammates look in the mirror, they're not ashamed of the face looking back at them.

-484-

Good teammates got your back, ever if you don't have theirs.

-485-

Good teammates are constantly on the lookout for opportunities to help.

-486-

Good teammates accept decisions that are best for the team.

-487-

Want your team to go from good to great? Start by finding a way to help your teammates get better.

-488-

Good teammates don't coast. They give their best effort for their team...*every* rep.

-489-

Good teammates must have the courage to confront.

-490-

Let kindness be your compass and your heart be your eyes.

-491-

Good teammates say what they mean without using mean words.

-492-

The path to healing can be found in the act of sharing.

-493-

Good teammates do the inconvenient things that help the team succeed.

-494-

When we share, we both equip and empower others.

-495-

Good teammates don't complain about things they aren't willing to try and change.

-496-

Nothing builds confidence like knowing you've got the support of your teammates.

-497-

Good teammates fight for their team's culture every day.

-498-

Commit to being better than you were yesterday.

-499-

A day is not complete without a chuckle, a tear, and a hug. Good teammates are often the source for all three.

-500-

Good teammates understand that victories come in many different forms.

-501-

Teammates who aren't committed have no future.

-502-

Good teammates refuse to compromise their standards.

-503-

True happiness is having one teammate with whom you can discuss anything.

-504-

Good teammates earn respect by having respect.

-505-

The team's transition from failure to success doesn't happen without the emergence of good teammates.

-506-

Good teammates practice like they've never won but perform like they've never lost.

-507-

Good teammates provide the beat to the team's tune.

-508-

Everything happens for a reason. Sometimes you need to be that reason.

-509-

Good teammates don't hurt, they heal.

-510-

Confidence breeds confidence. Your example is important.

-511-

Good teammates build unbreakable bonds.

-512-

Anyone who's ever played sports and had to run sprints understands the significance of "the line." Good teammates touch the line *every* time.

-513-

Being someone's teammate is a privilege.

-514-

Good teammates are on a mission: Serve the team.

-515-

Do unto your teammates as you would have them do unto you.

-516-

Good teammates stand strong in the face of adversity.

-517-

Good teammates derive their identity from their team's accomplishments.

-518-

Good teammates understand the difference between urgency and panic.

-519-

Attitude influences action.

-520-

Good teammates never allow distractions to cloud their vision.

-521-

Quality relationships are the trophies of good teammates.

-522-

The little engine who thinks he can…usually does.

-523-

Good teammates add light to a dark team.

-524-

Being a good teammate means understanding that growth comes in plateaus.

-525-

Good teammates approach the start of their day with a simple rule: Positive vibes only.

-526-

Unify your team through your example.

-527-

When you encourage, you empower and enlighten.

-528-

Good teammates must be bigger than the team's biggest problem.

-529-

The more influence you have, the greater your responsibility.

-530-

Good teammates cannot be afraid to be introspective.

-531-

To good teammates, humility means sacrificing your ego for the benefit of the team.

-532-

Anything worthwhile requires diligence.

-533-

Develop good teammates, and good teamwork will soon follow.

-534-

Being a good teammate requires attitude, action, and accountability.

-535-

You cannot convey love by condoning your teammates' destructive behavior.

-536-

Good teammates must be passionate about their mission.

-537-

When you have the patience to endure, you have the ability to conquer.

-538-

Good teammates always take time to mentor.

-539-

It's OK for a teammate to *be* a character, as long as they *have* character.

-540-

Good teammates demonstrate enthusiasm in all they do.

-541-

Humility binds us. Arrogance divides us.

-542-

Good teammates don't confuse obsessive, addictive behavior for passion.

-543-

When you resist coaching, you limit improvement.

-544-

Good teammates must eliminate the phrase "I told you so" from their vocabulary.

-545-

Even a single unselfish act can ignite change.

-546-

Good teammates must have the courage to confront the source of their team's dysfunction.

-547-

Those who err are human. Those who refuse to repeat their errors are good teammates.

-548-

Loyalty originates in the heart.

-549-

A good teammate's greatest compliment is to be trusted.

-550-

Measure your success by the value you bring to your team.

-551-

An honest teammate seeks to be both fair and fearless in speaking the truth.

-552-

Good teammates should always ignore those who try to discourage.

-553-

The four "E's" of being a good teammate: 1.) Effort, 2.) Energy, 3.) Enthusiasm, and 4.) Empathy.

-554-

Good teammates cannot have an entitled mindset.

-555-

Procrastination is a foreign word to a good teammate.

-556-

Choosing to be somebody's good teammate is choosing to make a difference in the world.

-557-

Show mercy. The break you give someone may be what keeps them from breaking.

-558-

Good teammates believe everyone on the team is important.

-559-

Good teammates make sure everyone on the team matters. And they make sure everyone knows it.

-560-

Individual sacrifice leads to group success.

-561-

Good teammates care about everything—except who gets the credit.

-562-

When it comes to approachability, good teammates have an open-door policy. They're always available.

-563-

Good teammates make others feel safe.

-564-

Create comfortable relationships with everyone on the team.

-565-

Good teammates learn from their mistakes.

-566-

Show you're fully committed by making the extra effort.

-567-

Good teammates strengthen their hearts by lifting the spirits of others.

-568-

When you adopt the mindset of a good teammate, you render yourself able to adapt to the challenges of your team.

-569-

Do not allow yourself to become the teammate who no longer cares. Apathy leads to agony.

-570-

Good teammates painstakingly care about others.

-571-

Good teammates are purpose-driven. They put their *why* before their *how, where, who,* or *what.*

-572-

When you treat people with respect, you convey love.

-573-

Good teammates have the mindset that if you are going to give, then give it your all.

-574-

A good teammate's interest and concern are both genuine.

-575-

Good teammates become role models by embracing their role on the team.

-576-

Sometimes cutting someone a break can mend your spirit.

-577-

Love is the fuel that powers a good teammate's heart.

-578-

Good teammates understand that it takes passion to make the impossible possible.

-579-

Being a good teammate is the only role shared by everyone on the team.

-580-

You gain ground by embracing the struggle to succeed.

-581-

Good teammates admit their mistakes and then go out of their way to right their wrongs.

-582-

A sense of humor is a sense of who you are.

-583-

Popularity is temporary. Being a good teammate is timeless.

-584-

Good teammates allow authenticity to bridge the gap between their actions and their words.

-585-

You must have the courage to face your flaws and the conviction to fix them.

-586-

Good teammates are often bigger on the inside than they are on the outside.

-587-

Talent is a gift. Being a good teammate is a choice.

-588-

Good teammates dig the team out of holes, not into them.

-589-

Good teammates have a tendency to be in the right place at the right time—because they *choose* to make it the right place and right time.

-590-

Consistent commitment defines a good teammate.

-591-

Good teammates are not complacent.

-592-

Being a good teammate is a calling.

-593-

Good teammates must be a treasure trove of inspiration.

-594-

What good teammates *do*, what they *say*, and what they *say they do* should all be trusted.

-595-

Good teammates don't dabble in kindness, they immerse themselves.

-596-

When you are driven by excellence, you're headed in the right direction.

-597-

Good teammates are virtuous.

-598-

The pursuit of *what is just* doesn't always lead to what is pleasant. Pursue *what is just* anyway.

-599-

Good teammates don't allow success to change their values.

-600-

Be mindful of others and others will not mind you.

-601-

Good teammates constantly evaluate their methods.

-602-

When you take responsibility for your choices, you show your commitment to improving.

-603-

Good teammates make being part of the team fun.

-604-

You can't be a good teammate if you are always consumed by insecurities.

-605-

Good teammates challenge excuses.

-606-

Being the best player means also being the best teammate. There should be no distinction between those two labels.

-607-

Good teammates develop their priorities by identifying what's best for their team.

-608-

When you know you are surrounded by good teammates, don't expect them to become you. You become them.

-609-

Good teammates are able to rejoice in the accomplishments of others.

-610-

Understand that the right way may not be the popular way.

-611-

Good teammates lift others through their example.

-612-

If left unmended, a broken spirit can break the team.

-613-

Be who you are...and not from afar. Don't allow those who criticize your integrity to cause you to be distant.

-614-

Duty and honor are inseparable to good teammates.

-615-

Having a big heart is more helpful than having a big ego.

-616-

Ethical teammates understand that pursuing success does not mean anything goes.

-617-

Good teammates allow others to feel like they can admit to making mistakes.

-618-

When good teammates err, they accept the blame.

-619-

Good teammates aspire to become the best version of themselves.

-620-

Invest in your talent, and you'll get ahead. Invest in your teammates' talent, and you'll ALL get ahead.

-621-

Good teammates are the flint that sparks the fire of success.

-622-

We cannot escape the fact that life is a team-oriented experience.

-623-

Good teammates care small but dream big.

-624-

When you own your mistakes, you gain equity in your honor.

-625-

Good teammates choose the better path over the bitter path.

-626-

Knowing the difference between *wants* and *needs* will determine the speed of your growth.

-627-

Good teammates understand that victories are often won before the game is played.

-628-

When it comes to problem solving, good teammates have a motto: *Talkin' ain't doing.*

-629-

Good teammates must be the team's driving force.

-630-

Become a phoenix by rising from adversity.

-631-

Good teammates know that bad times are relative when success is relevant.

-632-

A winning streak starts with a single victory, a change of attitude with a single thought.

-633-

Good teammates challenge others to reach their potential.

-634-

When the going gets tough, good teammates get going.

-635-

Good teammates understand that you are what you think.

-636-

Three Rules for Being a Good Teammate: 1.) Show up, 2.) Show out, and 3.) Don't show off.

-637-

Good teammates act until they achieve.

-638-

Choosing to be a better teammate can change life for the better.

-639-

Good teammates seek and nurture the talents of those around them.

-640-

Nothing good happens by accident. You must stay vigilant for opportunities and proactive in creating them.

-641-

Good teammates are the X-factor on their team.

-642-

Good teammates stay focused on team goals.

-643-

Success and poverty may be relative…but love is not.

-644-

Good teammates know the value of asking someone "What's your opinion?"

-645-

Unselfishness is vital to team culture, chemistry, and change.

-646-

Neutrality will destroy a team. Commitment will define it. Don't allow yourself to be a *fence-rider*.

-647-

Good teammates reject the status quo when it's counter to the team's culture.

-648-

Good teammates practice what they preach.

-649-

View your talents as a gift to your team.

-650-

Good teammates appreciate the people who push them to exceed their limits.

-651-

Good teammates are ultimately judged by what they give, not by what they receive.

-652-

Good teammates strive to make the leader's job easier.

-653-

Egos divide the team...*Let goes* bond it.

-654-

Good teammates understand how they practice is how they will play in the game.

-655-

The word *decommit* doesn't exist in the vocabulary of a good teammate. Once they commit, they stay committed.

-656-

Good teammates pursue team opportunities with passion and purpose.

-657-

When you're on a team, time is never yours, it's *ours*.

-658-

Good teammates choose to be unselfish, even when no one else on their team does.

-659-

Good teammates expect to do more than their share.

-660-

If the team needs, then so do you.

-661-

Good teammates play heart games, not head games.

-662-

A productive team culture is not a coincidence, it's the result of a choice.

-663-

Good teammates embrace challenges, and in doing so, they inspire confidence.

-664-

Good teammates do right, when it's right, because it's right.

-665-

Good teammates know that life is too important to be wasted on jealousy.

-666-

Inner peace comes from choosing to be a good teammate.

-667-

Good teammates are patient with everything—except toxic behavior.

-668-

Good teammates are as much aware as why they don't win, as they are of why they do.

-669-

Team milestones outweigh individual accolades.

-670-

Good teammates savor the smiles and laughter of those around them.

-671-

Give your best and don't stress about the rest.

-672-

If you can't be loyal, you can't be an effective teammate.

-673-

Good teammates must be principled people.

-674-

Be self-motivated, not self-righteous.

-675-

Good teammates must have a spirit of optimism.

-676-

Good teammates always set the tone.

-677-

Knowing the difference between confidence and arrogance is crucial to being a good teammate. One can save your team, the other can sink it.

-678-

You cannot fake being a good teammate. Your thoughts and actions must be genuine.

-679-

Good teammates savor every bit of the journey.

-680-

Good teammates weigh the value of their life by the impact it has on the lives of others.

-681-

When the darkness of doubt comes, good teammates must become the source of light.

-682-

Good teammates use past mistakes as learning tools.

-683-

Good teammates must be willing to point their finger at the person in the mirror.

-684-

The best individual awards stem from team success.

-685-

Good teammates don't allow themselves to burn out.

-686-

Good teammates are willing to break the unbroken to make it better.

-687-

When you encourage a culture of free-flowing thoughts, you foster innovation.

-688-

Question: What role are teammates willing to fulfill? Answer: Whatever role the team needs.

-689-

Good teammates donate their time to their team.

-690-

Good teammates push themselves and others—hard.

-691-

You must be willing to pivot to your team's needs.

-692-

Good teammate moves (i.e. acts of kindness, compassion, mercy, etc.) are what move the team forward.

-693-

Good teammates understand that confidence comes from the struggle. The struggle should not be feared.

-694-

A good teammate's convictions provide him with boundaries.

-695-

The attitude of a good teammate can make all the difference.

-696-

Good teammates elevate those around them by using what's within them.

-697-

Good teammates must be willing to overprepare.

-698-

If it can't be done with integrity, it shouldn't be done.

-699-

Good teammates take nothing for granted.

-700-

Being a good teammate starts with caring enough to be your team's hardest worker.

-701-

A good teammate's faith allows him to possess belief without evidence.

-702-

Good teammates understand that confidence comes from the struggle. The struggle should not be feared.

-703-

Good teammates must live their lives so that others want to emulate them.

-704-

Being a good teammate is a cause that demands relentless commitment.

-705-

Good teammates must have high hopes.

-706-

Good teammates have an unswerving desire to help others achieve.

-707-

You fail your team when you lack courage.

-708-

Good teammates are conduits that transfer vision to reality.

-709-

Good teammates invest in the people around them.

-710-

The view from the top is better when you look down and extend your hand to the next climber.

-711-

Good teammates are tough on the outside because they're strong on the inside.

-712-

Good teammates set their teammates up to succeed.

-713-

Perfection isn't a prerequisite for being a good teammate.

-714-

Good teammates will figure out what's important and act on it.

-715-

You elevate yourself when you help others leap their hurdles.

-716-

Good teammates are people magnets. Others are drawn to their kindness.

-717-

Make being a good teammate your life's work.

-718-

Good teammates are the antidote to a toxicity.

-719-

Praise from a good teammate is like a warm cup of cocoa on a chilly day.

-720-

Good teammates help others recognize and feel good about their achievements.

-721-

How you treat your teammates matters more than how they treat you. Ironically, the better you treat them, the better they will inevitably treat you.

-722-

Good teammates know their non-negotiables.

-723-

You win with good teammates.

-724-

Good teammates seek the truth and speak the truth.

-725-

Celebrate your victories! It will increase the likelihood of them being repeated.

-726-

Good teammates must be motivated by doing good.

-727-

Be sensitive to where your teammates are coming from by considering the context of their lives.

-728-

Good teammates facilitate group input.

-729-

The price of kindness is the sacrifice of comfort.

-730-

Good teammates inspire others to want to stand up and cheer.

-731-

Teams will never reach their potential until every member thinks and acts like a good teammate.

-732-

Good teams happen because of good teammates.

-733-

The truth guides a good teammate's decisions.

-734-

Good teammates inspire through hope, not fear.

-735-

Tough times challenge our convictions and test our commitment.

-736-

Good teammates are often defined by their response to inconvenience.

-737-

Your willingness to help is a glimpse into your values.

-738-

If it's important to their team, a good teammate will find a way.

-739-

By serving the team, good teammates become masters of themselves.

-740-

Good teammates never take more than they give.

-741-

He who harbors a slight will miss the haven of happiness.

-742-

Good teammates are beautiful because they choose not to dwell on the ugly.

-743-

A good teammate's story always ends with the words "Happily ever after…"

-744-

It's better to seek happiness than to chase pleasure.

-745-

Good teammates must dispense kindness and despise coldness.

-746-

Every moment is a golden moment for a good teammate.

-747-

Good teammates are not haunted by their regrets.

-748-

Both the letter and spirit of agreements matter greatly to good teammates.

-749-

Troubled is the teammate who chooses self over team.

-750-

Good teammates reduce grief by suggesting solutions when they present problems.

-751-

Toxic teammates are plagued by egotism.

-752-

Teams will unravel without unselfish teammates.

-753-

Superior teams are comprised of superior teammates.

-754-

Little things make a big difference when entrusted to good teammates.

-755-

Being thought of as a good teammate is to achieve team nobility.

-756-

Manipulation leads to resentment. Good teammates don't guilt others into acting.

-757-

Good teammates never sell themselves short.

-758-

The first step to building a good team is building good teammates. The frame of a team built without them will not be able to withstand the winds of selfishness.

-759-

Good teammates are passionate about being compassionate.

-760-

Peace of mind comes from preparation and organization.

-761-

Good teammates accept that they are what they are because of their own choices.

-762-

For teams, good times flow through good teammates.

-763-

Good teammates must live a goals-centered life, and their goals must be team-centered.

-764-

Kindness experiences no downtime when managed by good teammates.

-765-

Your most valuable asset is your love for your team.

-766-

Good teammates get joy by giving joy.

-767-

Good teammates seek the good in others for the good of their team.

-768-

Commit to fixing your flaws before they become habits.

-769-

Good teammates refuse to lose as a result of their repeated mistakes.

-770-

Overcome setbacks by being an unshakable optimist.

-771-

Good teammates operate with the mindset that the game is won when the job done.

-772-

Condemn those behaviors that condemn your team's culture.

-773-

Be a master of change instead of a prisoner of circumstances.

-774-

Good teammates grow their net worth by investing in their network.

-775-

Good teammates never stop paying their team dues.

-776-

Be loyal to those who sacrificed to put you in a position to be successful.

-777-

Embrace the premise that what is easy for you may be difficult for others.

-778-

Good teammates must be willing to solicit advice and heed advice.

-779-

Jealousy corrodes your heart.

-780-

Good teammates don't have to be *voluntold*.

-781-

If someone needs a mint, offer it. If someone offers you a mint, take it.

-782-

Good teammates are never confined by their comfort zones.

-783-

Successful teams are powered by synergy. Synergy is powered by unselfish teammates.

-784-

Be as committed to helping your teammates as you are to helping yourself.

-785-

If your standard is excellence, never settle for less.

-786-

Mindset matters. So mind the matter that enters you mind.

-787-

Competency is a requirement to being a good teammate.

-788-

Who gets the credit is of little concern to a good teammate, so long as the team succeeds.

-789-

Good teammates believe the power for change is within them.

-790-

When your teammate is in a better position to score than you, give them the ball.

-791-

The truth will set you free and bring your team closer together.

-792-

Half-assedness is a surefire method to fail.

-793-

Meaningful relationships aren't built through convenience.

-794-

Good teammates provide the framework for teamwork.

-795-

If you want a good life, surround yourself with good teammates.

-796-

Kindness echoes through history.

-797-

Unselfishness impacts the team's chemistry, culture, and cohesiveness.

-798-

Comfort zones are invisible cages that keep us from being better versions of ourselves.

-799-

See improving your talents as your gift to your team.

-800-

Blessed are those accompanied by good teammates.

-801-

Good teammates must hold themselves and everyone around them accountable.

-802-

Peace of mind comes from habitually doing the right thing.

-803-

Regarding their team's culture, good teammates must be perpetual marketeers.

-804-

Talent attracts talent. Hence, good teammates attract good teammates.

-805-

Good teammates must be self-motivated.

-806-

No team succeeds with half-way teammates.

-807-

Good teammates practice steadiness of purpose and readiness of service.

-808-

If having a *team-first* attitude doesn't make you indispensable, you're on the wrong team.

-809-

Good teammates do not require supervision.

-810-

Want to destroy a good teammate? Micromanage them. You will kill their selfless spirit.

-811-

Good teammates do not allow their convictions to be swayed by peer pressure.

-812-

Good teammates assert themselves through their example.

-813-

The required minimum is a good teammate's starting point.

-814-

Good teammates have to be irreproachable without being unapproachable.

-815-

Even a good teammate needs to know they're appreciated.

-816-

Good teammates push others on the team to become better versions of themselves.

-817-

Blind loyalty can prevent you from seeing reality.

-818-

Good teammates must always choose the hard right over the easy wrong.

-819-

You can't be bitter and be a good teammate. Let it go.

-820-

Good teammates are like coffee. They perk you up.

-821-

Better to be propelled by positivity than derailed by negativity.

-822-

You must believe in the mission before earning the right to question the strategy.

-823-

Good teammates don't create pollution with their inclusion.

-824-

A good teammate stands out because of what they exude from within.

-825-

Good teammates let their influence be their source of power.

-826-

Being a good teammate is not a one-time positive action, it is an ongoing positive habit.

-827-

A big heart must precede a big dream.

-828-

When your motives are driven by the needs of your team, your heart is void of a void.

-829-

Strive to understand before you commit to condemn.

-830-

A good teammate's nightly promise: Do better tomorrow.

-831-

What you have in common with your teammates must supersede your differences.

-832-

If you can't beat them, ~~join them~~...eliminate the word can't from your vocabulary.

-833-

Good teammates are tough—physically, mentally, and emotionally.

-834-

Enthusiasm—convey it, don't constrain it.

-835-

Good teammates are consumed with production, not obstruction.

-836-

It's essential for good teammates to prioritize self-sacrifice over self-preservation.

-837-

Listening leads to empathy.

-838-

Don't let leading by example be the extent of your leadership. Make your example be your starting line.

-839-

Grow your team by helping your teammates.

-840-

Bitter teammates rarely become better teammates.

-841-

Speak up before it's too late. Silence can lead to regret.

-842-

Good teammates are committed to systematic improvement.

-843-

Having a standard of personal excellence means not accepting anything less than your best.

-844-

Good teammates focus fully on whatever it is they are doing. They ignore distractions and deplore disruptions.

-845-

Curiosity allows good teammates to enlarge their sphere of knowledge and broaden their awareness.

-846-

Good teammates care enough to be eternally uplifting.

-847-

You don't have to be happy to be cheerful.

-848-

Good teammates take pride in being productive.

-849-

The only thing keeping lemons from becoming lemonade is our attitude.

-850-

Good teammates rarely need to be reminded to do anything but care enough to tactfully remind others.

-851-

When others feel empowered and confident because of you, you're a good teammate.

-852-

Good teammates listen with their ears and their eyes.

-853-

Do the right thing. Every time. Always. Forever. Perpetually.
No exceptions.

-854-

Good teammates must have the confidence to project bravery,
yet admit vulnerability.

-855-

Be someone's inspiration. It will impact both of your lives.

-856-

Good teammates always have love in their heart.

-857-

It's nice to know your opponents, but it's crucial to know
your teammates.

-858-

Believe in something bigger than yourself.

-859-

No greater honor exists within the confines of a team than to be labeled a good teammate.

-860-

Ignorance and arrogance disrupt your capacity to be a good teammate.

-861-

Never allow permanent goals to be furloughed by provisional success.

-862-

One can never have too many good teammates.

-863-

Good teammates must have the courage to encourage.

-864-

Be loyal to the loyal.

-865-

Good teammates can cultivate civility without compromising their character.

-866-

The best teammates know that material success is temporal but relationship success is eternal.

-867-

The company you keep parallels the harvest you reap.

-868-

If you work without an objective, you'll end up objecting to your work.

-869-

You must have the courage to act beyond your comfort zone.

-870-

When you compromise your values, you devalue your worth.

-871-

Good teammates keep their wits when others are having fits.

-872-

He who trusts the process never succumbs to unnecessary anxiety.

-873-

Good teammates must possess the sensitivity of a grandmother and the toughness of a Bering Sea fisherman.

-874-

When presented with options, choose the one that ensures your status as a bona fide good teammate.

-875-

Every day is a good day to be a good teammate!

-876-

Good teammates do not allow success to alter their ego.

-877-

Inspiration produces better results than fear. Good teammates lead with the carrot, not the stick.

-878-

If you're ill at ease with someone you consider to be a good teammate, reconsider your standards.

-879-

Good teammates never act out of malice or spite.

-880-

The teammate who believes achieves.

-881-

Good teammates don't allow themselves to fall into the trap of following mob mentality. Be strong in your convictions.

-882-

Your life will thrive when you invest in the lives of others.

-883-

Good teammates are bankable.

-884-

When your relationships are based on love, all of the other virtues fall into place.

-885-

Good players are respected. Good teammates are admired.

-886-

Teaching a child to be a good teammate can change the world.

-887-

Good teammates must be an instrument of inspiration.

-888-

Good teammates operate on a 3:1 ratio of compliments to criticism.

-889-

It is not binary. You can be a good teammate and be the best player on your team at the same time.

-890-

Good teammates love the labor of their trade.

-891-

Don't allow regrets to occupy space intended for dreams.

-892-

Good teammates are essentially tough-minded optimists.

-893-

You don't have to be a lion to roar.

-894-

Control your emotions. Team members who wear their emotions on their sleeve will soon find themselves changing jerseys.

-895-

Good teammates must devote uninterrupted chunks of time to their team.

-896-

Be an obliger of kindness.

-897-

Good teammates are defined by their habits.

-898-

There's nothing ordinary about a good teammate.

-899-

A good teammate's character is the same in the light as it is in the dark.

-900-

Being a good teammate isn't a *some-of-the-time* endeavor. It's an *all-of-the-time* mindset.

-901-

Good teammates are repulsed by repeated mistakes.

-902-

The acceptance of mediocrity leads to inevitable regret.

-903-

Good teammates are willing to trade individual glory for team victory.

-904-

Ego is an unnecessary barrier to team unity.

-905-

Good teammates attack complex problems with simple solutions.

-906-

Every tool in a good teammate's repertoire is formed from love.

-907-

Good teammates have the courage to act even when there is no guarantee of them getting the result they desire.

-908-

The needle is moved by your actions, not your thoughts.

-909-

A good teammate's confidence is rooted in their preparation.

-910-

Good teammates don't allow their teammates' confidence to be shaken.

-911-

Making others feel worthwhile increases your value.

-912-

Good teammates measure their success against their own potential.

-913-

Gentleness is a measure of inner-strength.

-914-

Good teammates must exude confidence and elude conceit.

-915-

Sometimes you must be your team's sunshine. Sometimes you must be your team's shade. Provide your team with what is needed.

-916-

Good teammates maintain their composure even when those around them aren't.

-917-

A team with good teammates can overcome any obstacle.

-918-

Good teammates help you think your best thoughts.

-919-

You grow selflessness by weeding selfishness.

-920-

Feed your soul with kindness and your kindness will feed others' souls.

-921-

Inspiring your teammates begins with your example.

-922-

Good teammates are *reassurers*. When your confidence wanes, they reassure you that the job can be done.

-923-

You don't have to be special to be a good teammate, but you won't be special until you are.

-924-

Good teammates are the fuel that powers good teams.

-925-

Inspire others to believe in their significance.

-926-

Good teammates know their example is more impactful than their advice.

-927-

Being a good teammate is like being pregnant—either you are or you aren't.

-928-

Good teammates never treat their subordinates as inferior.

-929-

Tolerating poor teammates leads to costly turnover.

-930-

Good teammates do not allow themselves to get too big to admit their mistakes.

-931-

Demand excellence from yourself before demanding it from others.

-932-

Nothing poses a bigger threat to team culture than selfishness.

-933-

Compromising integrity leads to the loss of credibility.

-934-

Good teammates treat problems like opportunities.

-935-

A teammate who resists being held accountable, cannot be counted on.

-936-

Good teammates use their talents to transform the selfish into the selfless.

-937-

Tenacity is a strategy employed by good teammates.

-938-

To be of value to your team, you must know when to step up and when to step back.

-939-

Being a faithful follower is a virtue.

-940-

The road to being a better teammate is always under construction.

-941-

Good teammates don't sulk, alibi, or make excuses.

-942-

If you have a problem with the attitude of someone you know is a good teammate, you are the problem.

-943-

Be receptive to exceptions. Just because you're often right doesn't mean you're always right.

-944-

If you build an alliance with a good teammate, you will never be let down.

-945-

Good teammates know the little things aren't so little.

-946-

Embrace teammates who seek your guidance.

-947-

Good teammates never tire of helping others succeed.

-948-

Good teammates don't object to being known as problem solvers.

-949-

You can't be a good teammate if you can't make sacrifices.

-950-

Good teammates don't compete against each other. They compete for each other.

-951-

How much you invest in your teammates is an indication of how deeply you care about your team.

-952-

Good teammates have the capacity to delay gratification.

-953-

Stress comes from trying to control that which you cannot control.

-954-

Good teammates are the antidote to the *disease of me*.

-955-

Never be too stubborn to say "I changed my mind" when you get new information.

-956-

Organize your life around your relationship with your team.

-957-

Good teammates see beyond their teammates' limits.

-958-

Accept responsibility for knowing what your team expects from you.

-959-

Denying your team full access to your talents limits your personal success and that of your team.

-960-

Good teammates are conquerors of selfishness.

-961-

Take pride in protecting the weaknesses and accentuating the strengths of your teammates.

-962-

To good teammates, nurturing relationships is a necessity.

-963-

You build a healthy team culture by eliminating purposeless habits.

-964-

Conflict does not compromise a good teammate's commitment.

-965-

Be consumed with the impact your life has on others.

-966-

Invested teammates are in it for the long haul.

-967-

Good teammates take pride in honoring their convictions.

-968-

No matter how many positive qualities you have, you will never be a good teammate if you lack character.

-969-

Good teammates never show frustration, fear, or fatigue.

-970-

Being a good teammate begins and ends with your commitment to your team.

-971-

Good teammates possess firmness of virtue.

-972-

Serving the needs of your team should be viewed as a blessing, never a burden.

-973-

Good teammates earn the right to lead by serving the needs of their team.

-974-

Never let a teammate with a good heart feel isolated or lonely.

-975-

Even one broken spoke will doom a wheel. Every member of the team is important.

-976-

Good teammates see purpose in their work. They don't lay bricks; they build cathedrals.

-977-

To provide hope to others is to be a good teammate.

-978-

Good teammates look beyond *what is* to see *what can be*.

-979-

Let your example liberate others from the confines of selfishness.

-980-

Vengeance cannot be the source of tough love.

-981-

Good teammates choose *finding a way* over *finding an excuse*.

-982-

Choosing what's best for the team instead of what's best for yourself is a sign of character.

-983-

A team in crisis is a team in need of good teammates.

-984-

Self-sacrifice should never lead to enabling your teammates' toxic behaviors.

-985-

Teams that need renovation don't always need better talent; sometimes they just need better teammates.

-986-

Standing firm in your faith facilitates hope.

-987-

Be the kind of teammate who is loathed by grouches.

-988-

Good teammates must be singular in purpose: Attend to the needs of the team.

-989-

Don't allow yourself to succumb to the curse of comparisons.

-990-

On many teams, the difference between a bond and a connection is the commitment of the teammate.

-991-

Good teammates communicate their values through their actions.

-992-

Selfishness is a good teammate's top adversary.

-993-

You protect your team's culture by projecting its values.

-994-

Good teammates do not cause grief for their leaders, their teammates, or themselves.

-995-

Selective hearing shields the team from elective destruction.

-996-

Be concerned with the contents of your teammates' hearts.

-997-

The sun never sets on a good teammate's kindness.

-998-

Good teammates want to be held accountable.

-999-

When crisis strikes, lean on your good teammates.

-1000-

Good teammates need to live their life in obedience to the needs of their team.

-1001-

No better compliment exists than to be remembered as a good teammate.

Bring the Good Teammate Message to Your Team

Are you interested in bringing the "Good Teammate" message to your event or implementing strategies to improve the quality of the teammates you have on your team? If so, contact Lance Loya's team at:

Phone: (814) 659-9605

E-mail: info@coachloya.com

Website: www.coachloya.com

Twitter: @coachlanceloya

Facebook: facebook.com/coachloya

LinkedIn: linkedin.com/in/coachloya

Join the movement and sign up for Lance Loya's weekly *Teammate Tuesday* blog at *www.coachloya.com/blog*.

*If you have enjoyed this book or it has inspired you in some way, we would love to hear from you! Be a good teammate and <u>share</u> your photos and stories with us through email or social media. We want to hear from you!

Also by Lance Loya

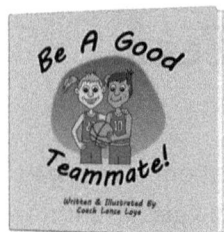

Be a Good Teammate

An illustrated children's book that teaches the importance of teamwork and how to be a good teammate. Good teammates care, share, and listen. You don't have to play sports to be on a team. This book encourages kindness and counters bullying.

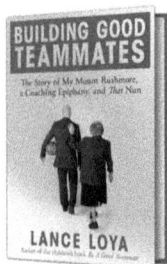

Building Good Teammates

The story of Lance Loya's discovery of an alternative approach to coaching players to be good teammates. Explore how his personal Mount Rushmore—the four men who had the biggest impact on his life—and a quirky nun influenced his coaching methodology.

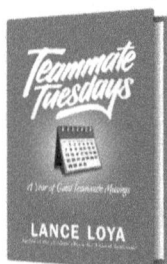

Teammate Tuesdays

A compilation of the entire first year of Lance Loya's popular weekly blog of the same name. Each chapter examines a different aspect of being a good teammate. Gain insight and encouragement through a variety of "good teammate" observations.

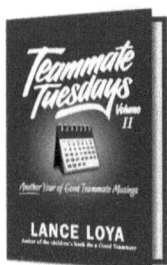

Teammate Tuesdays Vol. II

A compilation of another entire year of Lance Loya's popular weekly blog of the same name. Includes *musings* ranging from touching "good teammate" stories to creative ideas for inspiring team members to become better teammates.

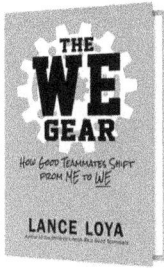

The WE Gear

Dive deep into the psyche of good teammates. Everybody wants teamwork on their team, but teamwork does not happen without good teammates—individuals whose unique way of thinking propels their team to success no matter what team they are on.

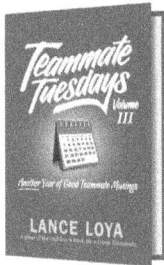

Teammate Tuesdays Vol. III

In this third installment of the *Teammate Tuesdays* series, Lance Loya once again chronicles a year of his journey exploring what it means to be a good teammate. Fifty-two weeks of observations unfold through fifty-two short, easily digestible chapters.

Learn from a Course

About the Author

Lance Loya is the founder and CEO of The Good Teammate Factory. He specializes in getting individuals to shift their focus from *me* to *we* and discover genuine purpose in their lives. Lance previously wrote the children's book *Be a Good Teammate* and the adult nonfiction titles *Building Good Teammates: The Story of My Mount Rushmore, a Coaching Epiphany, and That Nun*; *Teammate Tuesdays: A Year of Good Teammate Musings*; *Teammate Tuesdays Volume II: Another Year of Good Teammate Musings*, *The WE Gear: How Good Teammates Shift from Me to We*; and *Teammate Tuesdays Volume III: Another Year of Good Teammate Musings*.

A college basketball coach turned author, blogger, and professional speaker, he is known for his enthusiastic personality and his passion for turning *teambusters* into good teammates. He has inspired readers and audiences around the globe through his books, keynotes, and seminars.

When not speaking or writing, he is a loyal husband to his high school sweetheart and a doting father to his two daughters.

www.ingramcontent.com/pod-product-compliance
Lightning Source LLC
Chambersburg PA
CBHW060156070426
42447CB00033B/1501